ROSEN ✓ Verified
U.S. GOVERNMENT

THE BILL OF RIGHTS

Kathleen A. Klatte

Rosen
PUBLISHING

New York

Published in 2021 by The Rosen Publishing Group, Inc.
29 East 21st Street, New York, NY 10010

Editor: Siyavush Saidian
Book Design: Reann Nye

Photo Credits: Cover (background) selimaksan/iStock/Getty Images Plus/Getty Images; cover (Bill of Rights) Jack R Perry Photography/Shutterstock.com; series Art PinkPueblo/Shutterstock.com; p. 5 Charles Haire/Shutterstock.com; p. 6 Georgios Kollidas/Shutterstock.com; p. 7 eurobanks/Shutterstock.com; p. 9 J. Bicking/Shutterstock.com; p. 11 Smith Collection/Gado/Archive Photos/Getty Images; p. 12 Andrew Lichtenstein/Corbis News/Getty Images; p. 13 (Jefferson) https://commons.wikimedia.org/wiki/File:Official_Presidential_portrait_of_Thomas_Jefferson_(by_Rembrandt_Peale,_1800)(cropped).jpg; p. 13 (Monticello) DNY59/iStock Unreleased/Getty Images; p. 14 Marla Aufmuth/Getty Images Entertainment/Getty Images; p. 15 DisobeyArt/Shutterstock.com; pp. 16, 17 Anadolu Agency/Getty Images; p. 19 © iStockphoto.com/MachineHeadz; p. 20 Brian Goodman/Shutterstock.com; p. 21 PeopleImages/E+/Getty Images; p. 23 Zolnierek/Shutterstock.com; p. 25 moodboard/Brand X Pictures/Getty Images; pp. 26–27 Roman Motizov/Shutterstock.com; p. 29 John Mahler/Toronto Star/Getty Images; p. 31 ciud/Shutterstock.com; p. 32 Boudikka/Shutterstock.com; p. 33 robert cicchetti/Shutterstock.com; p. 34 MANDEL NGAN/AFP/Getty Images; p. 35 (Marshall) Cynthia Johnson/The LIFE Images Collection/Getty Images; p. 35 (O'Connor) Charles Ommanney/Getty Images News/Getty Images; pp. 35, 41 Everett Historical/Shutterstock.com; p. 37 David Attie/Michael Ochs Archives/Getty Images; pp. 38–39 Diego G Diaz/Shutterstock.com; pp. 42–43 KENA BETANCUR/AFP/Getty Images; p. 45 Ariel Skelley/DigitalVision/Getty Images.

Library of Congress Cataloging-in-Publication Data

Names: Klatte, Kathleen A., author.
Title: The Bill of Rights / Kathleen A. Klatte.
Description: New York : Rosen Publishing, 2021. | Series: Rosen Verified: U.S. government | Includes index.
Identifiers: LCCN 2019059412 | ISBN 9781499468519 (paperback) | ISBN 9781499468526 (library binding)
Subjects: LCSH: Civil rights—United States—Juvenile literature.
Classification: LCC KF4750 .K53 2021 | DDC 342.7303—dc23
LC record available at https://lccn.loc.gov/2019059412

Manufactured in the United States of America

Some of the images in this book illustrate individuals who are models. The depictions do not imply actual situations or events.

CPSIA Compliance Information: Batch #BSR20. For Further Information contact Rosen Publishing, New York, New York at 1-800-237-9932.

Find us on

CONTENTS

A LIVING DOCUMENT

The first ten **amendments** to the U.S. Constitution are called the Bill of Rights. But whose rights are we talking about? People's rights? States' rights? The **federal** government's rights? It's a complicated question. People have been arguing about it for more than 200 years.

The men who wrote the Constitution knew that ideas can change over time. Allowing for changes to be made was a good way to make sure that the Constitution would always protect everyone's rights.

The original Constitution didn't contain a clear list of people's individual rights. This upset many people. They wanted limits placed on the new government to protect their freedom. The Bill of Rights is the list of citizens' rights that are protected by federal law.

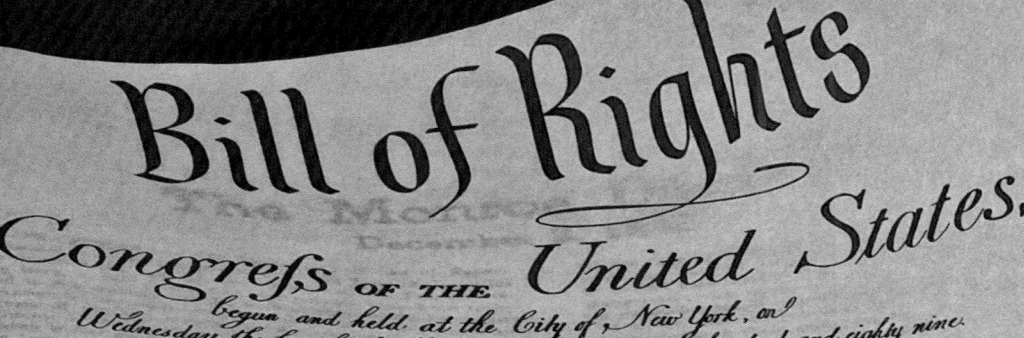

Bill of Rights

Congress OF THE United States,

begun and held at the City of, New York, on
Wednesday, the fourth of March, one thousand seven hundred and eighty nine.

The Bill of Rights was added to the U.S. Constitution in 1791.
The amendments were written by James Madison.

WHOSE IDEA WAS THIS?

The idea of limiting the power of government isn't new. In 1215, King John of England signed a document called the Magna Carta. It listed rights that the government gave the English people.

By the time of the American Revolution, the idea that all people had the same basic rights was spreading. So was the idea that people should have a say in their government. England, France, and some of their colonies had laws that listed people's rights.

VOLTAIRE

Voltaire was a famous French writer. He wrote and spoke about human rights. Those are rights that everyone, everywhere should have. The Founding Fathers probably read his books.

"We the people" sounds like it should mean "everyone." However, it took almost 200 years for "everyone" to include women and people of color.

IMPORTANT DOCUMENTS

1215: The Magna Carta

1689: The English Bill of Rights

1776: The Virginia Declaration of Rights

1789: The Declaration of the Rights of Man

1791: The Bill of Rights

WHAT'S AN AMENDMENT?

The Founding Fathers lived in a time when many things were being learned about the world. Lots of new ideas were spreading. They knew that America would change over time. Article V of the Constitution says that changes, or amendments, can be made.

An amendment to the Constitution is a law that affects everyone in the United States. For example, the 13th Amendment made slavery illegal. The 19th Amendment gave women the right to vote.

The Equal Rights Amendment (ERA) is a proposed amendment to the Constitution. It says that women should have the same rights as men.

COVERING ALL THE BASES

When the Constitution was first written, it didn't have a Bill of Rights. People felt that just saying "everyone has rights" wasn't good enough. They thought it was important to list exactly what their rights were under the new government. In fact, some states wouldn't accept the Constitution without a Bill of Rights.

People also wanted to limit the powers of the new government. They wanted to be sure that their new freedoms couldn't be taken away.

SOME OF THE CIVIL LIBERTIES LISTED IN THE VIRGINIA DECLARATION OF RIGHTS:

- Freedom of the press
- Freedom of religion
- Due process of the law

George Mason wrote the Virginia Declaration of Rights. It's one of the documents that the Constitution and the Bill of Rights are based on. Mason enslaved people, but he still thought the slave trade was wrong.

I'VE HEARD THINGS ABOUT THEM

Sometimes, people accept bad ideas for a long time. One of these ideas was slavery. That's the idea that people can own other human beings. The early economy of the United States was built on slave labor.

This is a re-creation of a cabin where enslaved people would have lived. It's also part of Monticello.

THOMAS JEFFERSON

Thomas Jefferson wrote the Declaration of Independence. He was president of the United States from 1801 to 1809. He's one of the people who insisted that the Constitution needed to have a Bill of Rights. He also enslaved Africans and had children with them. Do you think that should change the way people remember him?

This is Thomas Jefferson's home. It's called Monticello. It was built by enslaved people.

George Washington, Thomas Jefferson, and James Madison all enslaved Africans. African Americans weren't allowed to be citizens when the United States was founded. Today, people are still working to change old ideas that exist because of the history of slavery.

EXPRESS YOURSELF!

In your town, there are probably different kinds of places where people go to pray. There might be a big **cathedral**. There might also be a mosque or a temple. The First Amendment says that people can follow any religion they like—or none at all.

Think about places where you get **information**. Libraries, bookstores, and the internet contain all sorts of facts. The First Amendment also says that no one can control what people can read, watch, or listen to.

MALALA YOUSAFZAI

Malala Yousafzai is a young woman from Pakistan. She believes that girls have the right to go to school. She was shot by Taliban soldiers who disagree. Groups like the Taliban think that everyone must believe the same things that they do. The First Amendment exists so that things like this don't happen in the United States.

The First Amendment says that people can gather calmly to protest things they don't like. They can even pray in public if they want. They also have to respect the rights of people who don't agree with them.

A HOT TOPIC

The Second Amendment talks about "the right to bear arms." In this case, "arms" means weapons, or guns. This amendment raises lots of questions today.

Some people think it means they should be able to own guns to defend themselves. Other people say that's the job of the police.

✅ VERIFIED

The National Rifle Association (NRA) is a group that supports the right of law-abiding citizens to own guns. It lobbies for laws that support this idea. Its website is:
https://home.nra.org

Mass shootings are terrible **tragedies**. Many people say they could be prevented with stronger gun control laws. Others say owning guns is a constitutional right. What do you think?

Most people agree there should be laws about what kinds of guns people can buy or own. There are many fights about how strong those laws should be.

NOT IN MY HOUSE!

In **colonial** times, it was common for the British army to let its soldiers live in people's homes. American colonists were expected to feed and house the soldiers. They weren't paid for doing this.

The Third Amendment says this is against the law in the United States. There have never been any Supreme Court cases about this amendment. Today, some people think it's another **guarantee** of the right to privacy in their own homes.

The Third Amendment **involves** privacy in the home. Today, courts decide what this means for things like cell phones and the internet.

WHAT'S IT GOT TO DO WITH ME?

The Fourth Amendment says that police can't enter someone's home without good reason. They must have evidence of a suspected crime. They must also get a **warrant** from a judge. The warrant must say exactly what place can be searched. It also means that a person can't be searched without good reason.

The Fourth Amendment applies to everyone, even if they aren't U.S. citizens. Police or border officials can't enter a house without a warrant from a judge. It's important for people to know their rights.

FAST FACT

THE PATRIOT ACT WAS A RESULT OF THE **TERRORIST** ATTACKS OF SEPTEMBER 11, 2001. IT GAVE THE GOVERNMENT SPECIAL POWERS TO SEARCH FOR TERRORISTS. SOME CIVIL RIGHTS GROUPS THINK THESE POWERS ARE UNCONSTITUTIONAL.

Sometimes, the police think someone might be guilty of a crime because of the color of their skin. This is called racial profiling.

There have been many arguments about what this law applies to. Cars, photographs, phones, and computers didn't exist when the amendment was written.

THE REALLY IMPORTANT STUFF

The Fifth Amendment talks about people's rights if they're **accused** of a crime. Everyone has the right to due process of the law. This means that everyone deals with the same legal system.

People are innocent until proven guilty. This means that law enforcement officials must provide evidence against a person accused of a crime. A **jury** decides if there's enough evidence to prove that they're guilty. Then a judge decides a fair punishment.

DEFINING DUE PROCESS

- A person who's accused of a very serious crime has the right to a grand jury hearing. This jury decides if there's enough evidence for a trial.

- A person can't be tried twice for the same crime.

- A person doesn't have to give evidence against themselves.

- Everyone is entitled to the protection of the legal system.

- The government can't take private property without paying for it.

"Lady Justice" is shown blindfolded in artwork. This is because the law is meant to apply equally to everyone.

I SAW THAT ON TV!

The Sixth Amendment says that everyone has the right to a fair trial. Trials are often featured on TV crime shows. Everyone has the right to a trial by jury with a **lawyer** to help them. Everyone also has the right to know what they're accused of and who accused them.

Everyone has the right to an **impartial** jury. Many people are **interviewed** for a jury to be sure that they will treat the case fairly.

FAST FACT

FOR A LONG TIME, WOMEN WEREN'T ALLOWED TO SERVE ON JURIES. THE CIVIL RIGHTS ACT OF 1957 SAID WOMEN HAD THE RIGHT TO SERVE ON FEDERAL JURIES. HOWEVER, WOMEN COULDN'T DO SO IN MANY STATES UNTIL THE 1970s.

People are selected at random to receive a jury summons. This is a notice to report to a courthouse. Lawyers from both sides of a case question them. A good jury should have all sorts of different people.

PLEADING YOUR CASE

The Seventh Amendment says that people have the right to a jury trial in some civil cases. A civil case is a disagreement between two people or groups. It's not the same as a criminal case. A criminal case is when the government accuses someone of breaking the law.

It's common for civil cases to be settled without a trial. Sometimes, a judge decides the case. Sometimes, the people or their lawyers settle things without a trial.

In England at the time of the American Revolution, it was common for a judge to decide civil cases. This wasn't always fair.

FAIR AND JUST

The Eighth Amendment says penalties for crimes must be fair. Punishments must make sense for the crime that was committed. Judges also think about if the **convicted** person has committed a similar crime before.

Most people accused of a crime can pay money to be released from jail until their trial. This is called bail. The bail price must be fair for the crime the person is accused of. High bail should be set only when a crime is very serious.

Les Misérables is a famous story set in 1800s France. It's about a man who was sent to prison for years for stealing a loaf of bread. Does that sound like a fair punishment to you?

Actor playing Jean Valjean,
main character of *Les Misérables*

LEAVING ROOM TO GROW

Founding Father James Madison knew that he lived in a time of great change. There were many new inventions. He wanted the Constitution to be able to change with the times. The Ninth Amendment says that the freedoms listed in the Bill of Rights aren't the only rights that people are entitled to.

Over time, more amendments have been added to the Constitution. Judges have decided exactly what issues these amendments apply to.

FAST FACT

TODAY, THE RIGHTS OF TRANSGENDER AND NONBINARY PEOPLE ARE BEING QUESTIONED. JUDGES NEED TO FIGURE OUT HOW THE CONSTITUTION APPLIES TO THEM.

Inclusive bathroom laws have been the topic of discussions at both the state and federal level.

Many things have changed since the Constitution was written. These are some questions judges have considered in the last 200 years:

- Voting rights for African Americans, Native Americans, and women

- Women's reproductive rights

- Same-sex marriage

- Privacy of cell phones and email

- The rights of African Americans and women to serve in the armed forces

STATE VS. FEDERAL

The Tenth Amendment says that the federal government has only the powers listed in the Constitution. Any other powers are reserved for the states or for individuals. This was a way of limiting the reach of the government.

Some states get lots of snow every year. Others may get hurricanes and floods. Still others may have tornadoes or fires. It makes sense for the local government to decide what kind of equipment is best for dealing with local situations.

Federal laws apply to the whole country. The federal government does things like print money and declare war. Do you think it would make sense to have different kinds of money in each state? Should a state be able to declare war on another country?

The English government made laws for America from far away when it was under British rule. People didn't think this was fair. They wanted to have a say in their own government.

In the United States, state and local governments make decisions about things that affect their area. The federal government makes decisions that affect the entire country.

WHO DECIDES?

The Supreme Court is the highest court in the United States. It reviews cases that have gone through other courts. It also settles cases between states or between a state and the federal government.

The Supreme Court can rule that a state law is unconstitutional. Sometimes, it decides that something that used to be **legal** shouldn't be. It can also decide that some things that used to be illegal should be legal.

There are nine Supreme Court judges. They're chosen by the president and approved by the Senate. The head of the Supreme Court is called the chief justice.

SUPREME FIRSTS

John Jay

The first chief justice of the Supreme Court was John Jay. He was appointed by President George Washington. He served from 1789 to 1795.

Thurgood Marshall

Marshall was the first African American named to the Supreme Court. He was appointed by President Lyndon Johnson. He served from 1967 to 1991.

Sandra Day O'Connor

O'Connor was the first woman named to the Supreme Court. She was appointed by President Ronald Reagan. She served from 1981 to 2006.

WELL, IT LOOKS GOOD ON PAPER

For almost 200 years, the protections of the Bill of Rights were available only to men. This mainly meant white men who owned property. Slavery existed in the United States until 1865. Women didn't get the right to vote until 1920.

Passing laws to protect a group of people is only the beginning. Getting other groups to respect those laws can take a long time. Civil rights groups were formed to help people get the freedoms promised in the Constitution.

✅ VERIFIED

W. E. B. Du Bois was one of the founders of the National Association for the Advancement of Colored People (NAACP). The NAACP is the largest civil rights group in the United States. Its website is:
https://www.naacp.org

Civil rights activitists such as W. E. B. Du Bois have been responsible for making the laws of the United States more fair to racial, religious, and other minority groups.

CIVIL RIGHTS VICTORIES

1787: Constitution written

1791: Bill of Rights added to Constitution

1865: 13th Amendment ends slavery

1870: 15th Amendment grants African Americans the right to vote

1909: NAACP founded

1920: ACLU founded

1920: 19th Amendment grants women the right to vote

THE ACLU

The American Civil Liberties Union (ACLU) was formed in 1920. Its job is to make sure the Bill of Rights is applied fairly to everyone.

The ACLU has been involved in many court cases. The group has defended the rights to free speech and privacy. It has acted on behalf of **minorities**, as well as some very unpopular groups. Members believe everyone should have the same protection under the law. Its website is: **https://www.aclu.org**.

#AllFaithsWelcome

The ACLU protects the rights of people to protest peacefully. They make sure no one is arrested unless a law has been broken.

AND JUSTICE FOR ALL?

The Bill of Rights exists to protect everyone. This means all racial groups, including those who have been treated poorly, such as African Americans and Native Americans. These people weren't considered citizens when it was written. It covers all **immigrants**, who are owed forms of legal protection.

The Bill of Rights protects groups that say unpopular things. Even groups many people don't like can gather peacefully and speak freely. No one gets to decide whose rights are protected. "We the people" means everyone.

LEGAL UPS AND DOWNS

1868: The 14th Amendment grants African Americans equal protection under the law.

1896: *Plessy v. Ferguson* says "separate but equal" is legal.

1924: Congress declares Native Americans citizens.

1954: *Brown v. Board of Education* says school segregation isn't legal.

Segregation was the idea that African Americans couldn't use the same public places as white people. It used to be the law in some states.

WHAT IF?

There are places in the world where laws are based on religion. There are also places where a single ruler makes the law. This might mean books and music are restricted. It might also mean people must dress a certain way or behave a certain way in public.

Those are scary ideas. Think about living someplace where you're not allowed to go to a movie or play sports. The Bill of Rights protects U.S. citizens from this kind of government.

✓ VERIFIED

Amnesty International is an organization that defends human rights. It works to peacefully end injustice around the world. Its website is:
https://www.amnesty.org/en

WHY WE NEED THE BILL OF RIGHTS

The Constitution was never meant to be a finished document. The Founding Fathers allowed for ways that it could change over time. Amendments have been added as America has changed. In one case, an amendment was later **repealed**.

Today, judges interpret the Constitution in ways the Founding Fathers probably couldn't have imagined. *Roe v. Wade* is a very famous Supreme Court case. It says that a woman's reproductive rights are protected by the Bill of Rights. The ruling is based on the amendments that protect privacy.

After more than 200 years, people are still figuring out the Bill of Rights. Some still question the rights of other groups of people. It's a good thing that the Constitution has plenty of room to grow.

The best way to guarantee your own personal freedom is to vote! You should register to vote as soon as you're old enough.

GLOSSARY

accuse: To say that someone has done something wrong.

amendment: An official change to a document, such as the Constitution.

cathedral: A large church.

colonial: Related to the time of the 13 colonies that later became the United States.

convicted: Officially found guilty of a crime.

federal: Related to a national government.

guarantee: A promise of something.

immigrant: One who comes to a country to settle there.

impartial: Fair; able to treat things equally.

information: Facts about a subject.

interview: To question someone to find out more about them.

involves: Includes; talks about.

jury: A group of people picked from a large pool who make decisions on legal cases.

lawyer: A person who helps people in legal matters.

legal: Allowed by the law.

minority: A group of people who are a different race or have different beliefs from a larger group.

repeal: To officially say a law isn't valid anymore.

terrorist: A person who uses violence to send a message or support a belief.

tragedy: A very sad event.

warrant: An official court document that gives the police the power to do something.

INDEX